Ancient Sermons

for

Modern Times

By Asterius, Bishop of Amasia
Circa 375–405, A. D.

Put into English from the Greek
By
GALUSHA ANDERSON, S. T. D., LL. D.,
Professor of Homiletics, University of Chicago,
and
EDGAR JOHNSON GOODSPEED, Ph. D.,
Instructor in Biblical and Patristic Greek, University of Chicago

" As ye go, preach "

The Pilgrim Press
NEW YORK   BOSTON   CHICAGO

To those who have studied Homiletics under my direction and are now engaged in the peerless work of preaching Christ.

INTRODUCTION

FOUR or five years ago, while lecturing in the Divinity School of the University of Chicago on the History of Preaching, I spoke of the sermons of Asterius as especially interesting, and, although preached in the fourth century, as still fresh and admirably fitted to our times. Dr. Goodspeed, at that time a member of my class, and an enthusiastic and accurate Greek scholar, impressed by my remark, began to read some of the Greek discourses which I had so warmly commended. Convinced of their excellence, he made a literal translation of five of them. He chose for translation those sermons concerning whose authenticity there can scarcely be a reasonable doubt. Each of us went over this translation again and again, striving to present faithfully both the thought and spirit of the author, and at the same time to clothe his thought in clear and forceful English. All who have undertaken such a task, know how very difficult it is. How near we have come to the realization of our ideal the reader himself must judge.

Very little is known of the life of Asterius. We have no knowledge of his family. We have barely one fact concerning his early education. His principal teacher was a Scythian, who in his youth had been sold as a slave to a citizen of Antioch. His owner was a schoolmaster, and took great pains in educating him thoroughly. He made marvelous progress in learning and won for himself a great name among both Greeks and Romans. Under the immediate direction of this celebrated educator Asterius was trained for his life-work.

At some time, probably early in his career, he made a careful study of Demosthenes, and became himself no mean orator. He won popular favor. He was made Bishop of Amasia, in Pontus, Asia Minor. A few of his sermons there delivered have come down to us. They show rare rhetorical skill, a vivid and disciplined imagination, great power of expression, and, above all, intense moral conviction. He acted with the orthodox party of his day, and should be carefully distinguished from a contemporary of the same name, who was an Arian and a controversialist. He also has the reputation of having been a faithful pastor, one who earnestly devoted himself to the care of his flock. Moreover, his life was without a stain; his teaching and preaching were enforced by his godly living. Nor was his fame confined to the place where he preached publicly and from

house to house. During the iconoclastic
controversy, at the second council of
Nicæa, with a play on his name, he was
referred to as "a bright star illumining the
minds of all."

The limits of his public career are not
definitely known. He preached in the latter part of the fourth century and it may
be for a short time in the fifth. In his sermon, *On the Festival of the Calends*, he re-
fers to the fall of Eutropius from his consulship as an event of the preceding year;
now that event was in 399; this sermon
therefore was called forth by the festivities
of New Year's Day, A. D. 400. Elsewhere
Asterius spoke of himself as a man of ad-
vanced age, so that he probably did not
continue to preach long after the beginning
of the fifth century. So far as our knowledge extends that New Year's sermon
closed his career. He then historically

passed from view. What he did thereafter, no one in our day has ascertained. When, where and how he died is as yet wrapped in impenetrable mystery ; but he lives on in the very few of his many discourses that have survived the ravages of time. We have between twenty and thirty of them. Some scholars have doubted the authenticity of all that have been attributed to him, but he is in all probability the author of most of them. In addition to these discourses, with a high degree of plausibility, he has also been considered the author of a life of his predecessor, St. Basil of Amasia.

These five sermons, which we send out to the public in English dress, meet the altogether reasonable demand of our day for ethical preaching. In them moral subjects are handled with discrimination and with rare tact. This early Greek preacher laid right hold of the problems that were thrust

upon his attention by his immediate sur-
roundings and solved them by the applica-
tion of the immutable principles of righteousness, and the acknowledged truths of
the Word of God.   Measuring the conduct
of men by principles and truths universally
admitted, his discourses are as applicable to
men now as they were to those living in
the fourth century.   But he confined himself so strictly to topics purely ethical, that
we cannot but wish that he had treated
ethically some of the great fundamental doc-
trines of grace.   Still, in whatever respect
he may be justly criticized, all, we are sure,
will agree that he was a " live preacher."

We wish also to call attention to the fact
that since these sermons deal with men as
they were in the society of that early
period, they vividly present to us conditions and customs then prevailing among
the common people, that historians have

failed to portray. Moreover, these discourses are enriched with passages quoted from the Scriptures, which for the most part are suggestively and justly interpreted; so that the words of our author contribute something of value to our knowledge both of history and exegesis.

Asterius was a contemporary of Chrysostom; but while all of Chrysostom's sermons have been more than once translated into English, so far as we are aware this is the first time that any of the discourses of Asterius have appeared in our own tongue. And it will give us great pleasure, if, by this small volume, we shall be able to give to any one a larger knowledge of the early Greek pulpit, and at the same time incidentally to call attention to a striking evidence of the unity in thought and spirit of the believers of the fourth and twentieth centuries.

These sermons stand in the Greek without texts; but in conformity to the custom of our day, I have placed on the page preceding each discourse the Scripture which the preacher freely discussed. There is, however, one exception. In his sermon, *On the Festival of the Calends*, he expounded no passage of Scripture. Like Chrysostom in his *Homilies of the Statues*, he seized upon a passing event, making that the foundation of his discourse, and with great force castigated a crying evil.

Last of all we wish to call special attention to the fact that these discourses are genuine sermons. They are at the farthest possible remove from essays. They were spoken directly to men. The preacher frequently said " you." He also often interrogated those to whom he spoke. He abundantly illustrated his thought. He appealed to reason; he pinched the conscience; he ridiculed folly; he shamed vice; he allured to virtue. He was not, to be sure, faultless, but in many respects he is a fine homiletical model, that will richly repay thoughtful study.

The Greek text from which these sermons were translated is found in Migne's Library of the Greek and Latin fathers.

GALUSHA ANDERSON.

Newton Centre, March 1, 1904.

CONTENTS

I

THE RICH MAN AND LAZARUS

There was a certain rich man, which was clothed in purple and fine linen, and fared sumptuously every day:

And there was a certain beggar named Lazarus, which was laid at his gate, full of sores,

And desiring to be fed with the crumbs which fell from the rich man's table: moreover the dogs came and licked his sores.

And it came to pass, that the beggar died, and was carried by the angels into Abraham's bosom: the rich man also died, and was buried;

And in hell he lift up his eyes, being in torments, and seeth Abraham afar off, and Lazarus in his bosom.

And he cried and said, Father Abraham, have mercy on me, and send Lazarus, that he may dip the tip of his finger in water, and cool my tongue; for I am tormented in this flame.

But Abraham said, Son, remember that thou in thy lifetime receivedst thy good things, and likewise Lazarus evil things; but now he is comforted, and thou art tormented.

And beside all this, between us and you there is a great gulf fixed: so that they which would pass from hence to you cannot; neither can they pass to us, that would come from thence.—*Luke 16 · 19–26.*

I

THE RICH MAN AND LAZARUS

OUR God and Saviour does not lead men to hate wickedness and love virtue by negative precepts alone, but also by examples he makes clear the lessons of good conduct, bringing us both by deeds and words to the apprehension of a good and godly life. As he has often told us by the mouths of both prophets and evangelists, nay, even by his own voice also, that he turns away from the overbearing and haughty man of wealth, and loves a kindly disposition, and poverty when united to righteousness ; so also in this parable, in order to confirm his teaching, he brings effective examples to attest the word, and in the narrative of the rich man and the

beggar points out the lavish enjoyment of
the one, the straitened life of the other,
and the end to which each finally came,
in order that we, having discerned the
truth from the practices of others, may
justly judge our own lives.

There was a rich man who was clothed
in purple and fine linen.[1] By two brief
words the Scripture ridicules and satirizes
the prodigal and unmeasured wastefulness
of those who are wickedly rich.   For purple is an expensive and superfluous color,
and fine linen is not necessary.   It is the
nature and delight of those that choose a
well-ordered and frugal life to measure the
use of necessary things by the need of
them; and to avoid the rubbish of empty
vainglory and deceptive amusement as the
mother of wickedness.   And that we may
see more clearly the meaning and force of

[1] Luke 16: 19.

this teaching, let us note the original use of clothing; to what extent it is to be employed when kept within rational limits.

What, then, says the law of the Just One?   Sheep God created with well-fleeced skins, abounding in wool.   Take them, shear it off, and give it to a skilful weaver, and fashion for yourself tunic and mantle that you may escape both the distress of winter, and the harm of the sun's burning rays.   But if you need for greater comfort lighter clothing in the time of summer, God has given the use of flax, and it is very easy for you to get from it a becoming covering, that at once clothes and refreshes you by its lightness.   And while enjoying these garments, give thanks to the Creator that he has not only made us, but has also provided for us comfort and security in living; but if, rejecting the sheep and the wool, the needful provision

of the Creator of all things, and departing
from rational custom through vain devices
and capricious desires, you seek out fine
linen, and gather the threads of the Persian
worms and weave the spider's airy web;
and going to the dyer, pay large prices in
order that he may fish the shell-fish out of
the sea and stain the garment with the
blood of the creature,—this is the act of a
man surfeited, who misuses his substance,
having no place to pour out the superfluity
of his wealth. For this in the Gospel such
a man is scourged, being portrayed as
stupid and womanish, adorning himself
with the embellishments of wretched
girls.

Others again, according to common report are lovers of like vanity; but having
cherished wickedness to a greater degree,
they have not restricted their foolish inven-
tion even to the things already mentioned;

but having found some idle and extravagant style of weaving, which by the twining of the warp and the woof, produces the effect of a picture, and imprints upon their robes the forms of all creatures, they artfully produce, both for themselves and for their wives and children, clothing beflowered and wrought with ten thousand objects. Thenceforth they become self-confident. They no longer engage in serious business; from the vastness of their wealth they misuse life, by not using it;[1] they act contrary to Paul and contend against the divinely inspired voices,[2] not by words, but by deeds. For what he by word forbade, these men by their deeds support and confirm. When, therefore, they dress themselves and appear in public, they look like pictured walls in the eyes of those that meet them. And per-

[1] 1 Corinthians 7: 31.   [2] 1 Timothy 2: 9, 10.

haps even the children surround them, smiling to one another and pointing out with the finger the picture on the garment; and walk along after them, following them for a long time. On these garments are lions and leopards; bears and bulls and dogs; woods and rocks and hunters; and all attempts to imitate nature by painting. For it was necessary, as it seems, to adorn not only their houses, but finally also their tunics and their mantles.

But such rich men and women as are more pious, have gathered up the gospel history and turned it over to the weavers; I mean Christ himself with all the disciples, and each of the miracles, as recorded in the Gospel. You may see the wedding of Galilee, and the water-pots; the paralytic carrying his bed on his shoulders; the blind man being healed with the clay; the woman with the bloody issue, taking hold of the

border of the garment; the sinful woman
falling at the feet of Jesus; Lazarus return-
ing to life from the grave.   In doing this
they consider that they are acting piously
and are clad in garments pleasing to God.
But if they take my advice let them sell
those clothes and honor the living image
of God.   Do not picture Christ on your
garments.   It is enough that he once suffered the humiliation of dwelling in a human body which of his own accord he
assumed for our sakes.   So, not upon your
robes but upon your soul carry about his
image.

Do not portray the paralytic on your
garments, but seek out him that lies sick.
Do not tell continually the story of the
woman with the bloody issue, but have
pity on the straitened widow.   Do not
contemplate the sinful woman kneeling before the Lord, but, with contrition for your

own faults, shed copious tears. Do not sketch Lazarus rising from the dead, but see to it that you attain to the resurrection of the just. Do not carry the blind man about on your clothing, but by your good deeds comfort the living, who has been deprived of sight. Do not paint to the life the baskets of fragments that remained, but feed the hungry. Do not carry upon your mantles the water-pots which were filled in Cana of Galilee, but give the thirsty drink. Thus we have profited by the magnificent raiment of the rich man.

What follows must not, however, be overlooked; for there is added to the purple and fine linen, that he fared sumptuously every day. For of course both the adorning of one's self with useless magnificence, and serving the belly and the palate luxuriously, belong to the same disposition.

Luxuriousness, then, is a thing hostile to

virtuous life, but characteristic of idleness and inconsiderate wastefulness, of unmeasured enjoyment and slavish habit. And though at first blush it may seem a simple matter, it proves upon careful investigation to include manifold, great and many-headed evils. Luxuriousness would be impossible without great wealth; but to heap up riches without sin is also impossible; unless indeed it happens to some one rarely, as to Job, both to be abundantly rich, and at the same time to live in exact accord with justice. The man who will give himself to luxury, then, needs first a costly home, adorned like a bride, with gems and marbles and gold, and well adapted to the changes of the seasons of the year. For a dwelling is required that is warm, comfortable in winter, and turned toward the brightness of the south; but open toward the north in the summer, that

it may be fanned by northern breezes, light
and cool.　Besides this, expensive stuffs are
demanded to cover the seats, the couches,
the beds, the doors.　For the rich carefully
adorn all things, even things inanimate,
while the poor are pitiably naked.　Moreover, enumerate the gold and silver vessels,
the costly birds from Phasis, wines from
Phœnicia, which the vines of Tyre produce
in abundance and at a high price, for the
rich ; and all the rest of the wasteful equip-
ment which only those who use it can name
with particularity.

Now luxury, steadily increasing in elab-
orateness, even mingles Indian spices with
the food ; and the apothecaries furnish supplies to the cooks rather than to the physicians.　Then consider the multitude that
serve the table,—the table-setters, the cup-
bearers, the stewardesses and the musicians
that go before them, women musicians,

dancing girls, flute-players, jesters, flatterers, parasites,—the rabble that follows vanity. That these things may be gained, how many poor are robbed! how many orphans maltreated! how many widows weep! how many, dreadfully tortured, are driven to suicide!

Like one who has tasted some Lethean stream, the self-indulgent soul absolutely forgets what it itself is, and the body to which it has been joined, and that some day it shall be released from this union, and again at some future time inhabit the reconstructed body. But when the appointed time shall come, and the inexorable command separates the soul from the body, then also shall come the recollection of things done in the past life, and vain repentance, too late! For repentance helps when the penitent has power of amendment, but the possibility of reform being taken away, grief is useless and repentance vain.

There was a certain beggar named Lazarus. The narrative describes him not simply as poor, destitute of money, and of the necessaries of life, but also as afflicted with a painful disease, emaciated in body, houseless, homeless, incurable, cast down at the rich man's gate. And very carefully the narrative finally works up the circumstances of the beggar to signalize the hard-heartedness of him who had no pity; for the man that has no feeling of pity or sympathy for hunger or disease is an unreasoning wild beast in human form, deliberately and wickedly deceiving men; nay more, he is less sympathetic than the very beasts themselves; since, at least, when a hog is slaughtered, the rest of the drove feel some painful sensation and grunt miserably over the freshly spilled

blood; and the cattle that stand about
when the bull is killed indicate their distress by passionate lowing. Flocks of
cranes also when one of their mates is
caught in the nets, flutter about him and
fill the air with a sort of grieving clamor,
seeking to release their mate and fellow.
And how unnatural that man, endowed
with reason and blessed with culture, who
has also been taught goodness by the example of God, should take so little thought
of his kinsman in pain and misfortune!

So the suffering but grateful pauper lay
without feet, or else certainly he would have
fled from the accursed and haughty man,
and sought another place instead of the
inhospitable gate, which was closed against
the poor; he lay without hands, having not
even a palm to stretch forth for alms; his
very organs of speech were so impaired
that his voice was hoarse and harsh; in fact,

he was quite mutilated in all his members, the wreck of a foul disease, a pitiable illustration of human infirmity.[1] Yet not even such a list of misfortunes moved the haughty man to attention, but he passed the beggar as if he were a stone, deliberately filling up the measure of his sin; for, if accused, he could not utter this common and specious excuse, "I did not know: I was not aware: I did not notice the beggar howling." For the beggar lay before his gate, a spectacle as he went in and out to make the condemnation of the proud man inevitable. He was even denied the crumbs from the table; and while the rich man was bursting with fulness, he was wasting away with want. Therefore it would have been fair and right to have made the Canaanitish Phœnician woman the teacher of the mis-

[1] The disease of Lazarus is here represented as leprosy.

anthropic man of wealth, saying those things that are written : " Haughty wretch, even the dogs eat of the crumbs which fall from their masters' table,[1] and did you not think your brother, one who belongs to the same race, worthy of that bounty ? " But the dogs were carefully fed, the watch-dogs by themselves and the hunting-dogs by themselves, and they were deemed worthy of a roof, and beds and attendants were carefully allotted to them ; but the image of God was cast on the earth uncared for and trampled on,—that image which the great Builder and Maker of all fashioned with his own hand, if one regards Moses as having given credible testimony to the genesis of man.

Now if the story of Lazarus had ended at this point, and the nature of things were such that our life was truly represented by

[1] Matthew 15 : 27.

the inequality of his career with that of the rich man, I should have cried aloud with indignation,—that we who are created equal, live on such unequal terms with men of the same race. But since that which remains is good to hear, do you, poor man, who groan over the past, take courage from the sequel, when you learn the blessed enjoyment of your fellow in poverty. For you will find that the just Judge renders exact judgment, so that the man who has lived a life of ease groans, and he who has had hardship finds luxury, each receiving his due reward.

And it came to pass that the beggar died and was carried away by the angels into Abraham's bosom. Do you see who they were who ministered to the poor and just man, and who took him to heaven? For angels were his body-guard, looking upon him gently and mildly, and betokening by their manner the attendance and relief that awaited him. And he was taken and placed in the bosom of the patriarch, a statement which affords ground for doubt to those who like to question minutely the deep things of the Scriptures, for if every just man, when he dies, should be taken to the same place, the bosom would be a great one and expanded to an endless extent, if it were intended to accommodate the whole multitude of the saints. But if this is absolutely impossible—for the bosom can scarcely embrace one man and hardly two infants,—the thought presents itself to us that the material bosom is the symbol of a spiritual truth; for what is it that is meant? Abraham, he says, receives those who have lived an upright life. Then tell us, wonderful Luke,—for I will address you as though visibly present,—why, when there were many just men, even older than Abraham, did you withhold this distinction from his predecessors, passing in silence over Enoch, Noah and many others who were like these in their manner of life? But perhaps I understand you, and my judgment does not go wide of the mark. For Abraham was a minister of Christ, and, beyond other men, received the things of the revelation of Christ, and the mystery of the Trinity was adequately bodied forth in the tent of this old man when he entertained the three angels as wayfaring men. In short, after many mystical enigmas, he became the friend of God, who in after time put on flesh and, through the medium of this human veil, openly associated with men. On this account, Christ says that Abraham's bosom is a sort of fair haven, and sheltered resting-place for the just. For we all have our salvation and expectation of the life to come, in Christ, who, in his

human descent, sprang from the flesh of
Abraham. And I think the honor in the
case of this old man has reference to the
Saviour, who is the judge and rewarder of
virtue, and who calls the just with a gracious
voice, saying : " Come, ye blessed of my Father, inherit the kingdom prepared for you." [1]

And it came to pass that the beggar died.
Two sides of the beggar's life are indicated :
on the one hand is shown his poverty, and
on the other his modesty and the humility
of his character. Let not, therefore, the
man who is without substance, in want of
money, and clothed in pitiable garb appropriate to himself the praise of virtue,
nor think that want will secure for him salvation. For not he who is poor from
necessity is commended, but he is held up
to admiration who of his own accord
moderates his desires. For the poverty of

[1] Matthew 25 : 34.

those who are in extreme want, and have
at the same time an unmanageable or incor-
rigible disposition, leads to many evil deeds
of daring.   Whenever I have come near a
ruler's judgment-seat, I have seen that all
housebreakers and kidnappers, thieves and
robbers, and even murderers, were poor
men, unknown, houseless and hearthless.
So that from this it is clear that the Scripture accounts that poor man happy who
bears his hardships with a philosophic
mind, and shows himself nobly steadfast
in the face of his circumstances in life,
and does not wickedly do any evil deed to
gain for himself the enjoyment of luxury.
Such a man the Lord describes even more
clearly in the first of the beatitudes, where
he says : " Blessed are the poor in spirit." [1]
So, not every poor man is righteous, but
only one who is like Lazarus ; nor is every

[1] Matthew 5 : 3.

rich man to be despaired of, but only one who has the disposition of him that neglected Lazarus; and in real life we easily find witnesses of this truth. For who is richer than was the godly Job? Nevertheless his great prosperity did not divorce him from righteousness nor, to speak briefly, did it estrange him from virtue. Who is poorer than was Iscariot? His poverty did not secure salvation for him; but while associating with the eleven poor men who loved wisdom, and with the Lord himself, who for our sakes voluntarily became poor,[1] he was carried away by the wickedness of his covetous disposition and finally was guilty even of the betrayal.

It is also worth while to examine intelligently how each of these men when dead was carried forth. The poor man when he fell asleep had angels as his guards and

[1] 2 Corinthians 8: 9.

attendants, who carried him, full of joyful
expectation, to the place of rest; and the
rich man, Christ says, died and was buried.
It is not possible in any respect to improve
the declaration of the Scriptures, since a
single sentence adequately indicates the
unhonored decease of the rich man. For
the sinner when he dies is indeed buried,
being earthy in body, and worldly in soul.
He debases the spiritual within him to the
material by yielding to the enticements of
the flesh, leaving behind no good memorial
of his life, but, dying the death of beasts, is
wrapped in unhonored forgetfulness. For
the grave holds the body, and Hades the
soul,—two gloomy prisons dividing between
them the punishment of the wicked. And
who would not blame the wretched man for
his thoughtlessness ?—since when he was on
earth he prided himself, held his head high,
exulted over all who lived about him and

were of the same race, deeming those whom he chanced to meet hardly better than ants and worms, and vainly boasting of his short-lived glory. But when he dies, and like a scourged slave is deprived of those usurped possessions of which in his folly he thought himself master, he is as deeply humiliated as he was previously highly exalted, and, uttering complaints like a lamenting old woman, calls loudly and vainly on the patriarch, saying, " Father Abraham, have mercy on me, and send Lazarus, that he may dip the tip of his finger in water, and cool my tongue; for I am tormented in this flame." He seeks mercy, which he had not given when he had the power of benefiting another, and demands that Lazarus shall come down into the fire to him to help him. He prays that he may suck the finger of the leper slightly moistened in water. Such is

the thoughtlessness of those who love the
body. This is the end of those who love
wealth and pleasure. It therefore becomes
the wise man who is provident of the
future, to consider the parable as a sort of
medicine, preventive of sickness; and to
flee the experience of like evil, preferring
the sympathetic and philanthropic disposition as the condition of the life to come.
For the Scripture has presented the admonition to us dramatically in the persons of
particular characters in order to impress
upon us by a concrete and vivid example
the law of good conduct, so that we may
never think lightly of the precepts of the
Scripture as terrifying in word only, without
inflicting the threatened punishment. I
know that most men, snared by such
fancies, take the liberty of sinning. But
the Scripture before us teaches quite the
contrary, that neither any confession of

the justice of the judgment lightens the punishment, nor does pity for the one in torment lessen the penalty ordained; if indeed it is necessary that the Scripture attest the word of the patriarch. For after the manifold supplications of the rich man, and after hearing countless piteous appeals, Abraham was neither moved by the laments of the suppliant, nor did he remove from his pain the one who was bitterly scourged; but with austere mind he confirmed the final judgment, saying that God had allotted to each according to his desert. And he said to the rich man, Since in life you lived in luxury through the calamities of others, what you are suffering is imposed upon you as the penalty of your sin. But to him who once had hardships, and was trampled on and endured in bitterness life in the flesh, there is allotted here a sweet and joyful existence.

And besides, he says, There is also a great gulf which prevents them from intercourse with one another, and separates those who are being punished from those who are being honored, that they may live apart from each other, not mixing the rewards of good and evil deeds. And I suppose the parable to be a material representation of a spiritual truth. For let us not imagine that there is in reality a ditch digged by angels, like the trenches on the outer borders of military camps, but Luke by the similitude of a gulf has represented for us the separation of those who have lived virtuously and those who have lived otherwise. And this thought Isaiah also stamps for us with his approval, speaking somewhat thus : Is the hand of the Lord not strong to save, or is his ear heavy that it cannot hear ? But our sins stand between us and God.[1]

[1] Isaiah (59 : 1, 2) Lxx.

II

THE UNJUST STEWARD

And he said also unto his disciples, There was a certain rich man, which had a steward; and the same was accused unto him that he had wasted his goods.

And he called him, and said unto him, How is it that I hear this of thee? give an account of thy stewardship; for thou mayest be no longer steward.

Then the steward said within himself, What shall I do? for my lord taketh away from me the stewardship: I cannot dig; to beg I am ashamed.

I am resolved what to do, that, when I am put out of the stewardship, they may receive me into their houses.

So he called every one of his lord's debtors unto him, and said unto the first, How much owest thou unto my lord?

And he said, An hundred measures of oil. And he said unto him, Take thy bill, and sit down quickly, and write fifty.

Then said he to another, And how much owest thou? And he said, An hundred measures of wheat. And he said unto him, Take thy bill, and write fourscore.

And the lord commended the unjust steward, because he had done wisely: for the children of this world are in their generation wiser than the children of light.

And I say unto you, Make to yourselves friends of the mammon of unrighteousness; that, when ye fail, they may receive you into everlasting habitations.

He that is faithful in that which is least is faithful also in much: and he that is unjust in the least is unjust also in much.

If therefore ye have not been faithful in the unrighteous mammon, who will commit to your trust the true riches?

And if ye have not been faithful in that which is another man's, who shall give you that which is your own?
—*Luke 16: 1-12.*

II

THE UNJUST STEWARD

I HAVE often said to you in my discourses, that there is one fictitious and false conception prevalent among men, which multiplies their transgressions, and diminishes the good which we ought, each of us, to do. And this false conception is, that all that we have to enjoy in this life we possess as lords and masters. And on account of this notion we do fiercely fight and war and contend for it and protect it to the uttermost as a precious possession. Now the truth of the matter is not so, but quite otherwise. For none of those things which we have received is our own, nor do we as absolute possessors and lords dwell in this life as in a house of our own; but as sojourners, and strangers, and wanderers, and when we do not expect it, we are led whither we would not go. And when it seems good to the Lord we are deprived of the possession of our wealth. Wherefore the enjoyment of this perishable life is very liable to change. He who is to-day glorious, is to-morrow an object of pity, eliciting compassion and help. He who is now prosperous and flourishing in wealth, suddenly finds himself poor, without even bread to support life. In this respect especially does our God surpass mortals, in that he is always the same, and in the same state, and possesses life and glory and power inalienable.

Why I have thus begun my discourse, is perhaps already perceived by those who are attentive and intelligent. Luke has fashioned us a parable that, by way of preface, was just now read to us, in which he describes the steward of other men's goods as groaning and troubled, because, being luxurious and extravagant, he has heard from the master of the money and property, the words, "Give an account of thy stewardship and depart, for I will not suffer thee to revel in my possessions, as though they were thine own." Now this is not the narrative of a thing that really took place, but the fiction of a parable, which by obscure sayings inculcates moral virtue. Know then, that each one of you is an administrator of what belongs to another; cast off then the pride of authority, and put on the humility and prudence of a steward, accountable for his acts. Be always waiting for your Lord, to whom with fear you must render a strict account. For you are a sojourner who has received the privilege of only a temporary and fleeting use of the things in your possession.

And if you are in doubt about this, observe what happens, and be taught by experience, that trustworthy teacher.

You possess an estate, having either inherited it from your fathers, or obtained it by some exchange. Call up therefore in memory and count over, if you can, all who have occupied it before you. And direct your mind also to the time to come, and think how many are to occupy it after you. Then tell me who owns it, and to whom does it especially belong; those who have had it, or those who now have it, or those who in the future are to have it? For if some one should in some way or other call them all together, the owners would be found more numerous than the clods. And, further, if you wish to see exactly what our life is like, call to mind if ever in summer, while traveling, you have seen a flourishing tree extending far enough in breadth and height to serve with its shadow the purpose of a shelter. You were glad to come under its shade, and there you remained as long as possible. And when it was necessary to move on, even as you were thinking of setting off again, another wayfarer appeared. And you took up your luggage while he laid his down and appropriated all your conveniences, the bed of leaves, the fire, the shade of the tree, the water flowing by. And he began to recline and rest, while you resumed your walk. He, too, enjoyed the place and then left it. And that one tree was, in a single day, the temporary lodging-place for perhaps ten strangers. And that which was enjoyed by all belonged to but one owner. And thus also the abundance of our life here delights and supports many, while it belongs to God alone, who has imperishable and indestructible life.

You can call to mind an inn where, when traveling, you have put up. There, as you brought nothing with you, you were provided with many things, bed, table, drinking-cups, a plate and other dishes of all sorts. But perhaps before you had used them as long as you wished, another came, panting, covered with dust and hard after you, forcing you from the inn and demanding as though they were his own the things that really belonged to neither of you.

Such, brethren, is our life, and, if anything, it is still more transitory than the things I have mentioned. And I wonder at the way men say, " *my* estate," and " *my* house," and thus appropriate by an idle syllable things which are not theirs, and, with two deceptive letters, clutch things belonging to others. For as on the stage no one actor has exclusive right to any given character, but any actor may assume

it, so is it in the case of the earth and its
material things. Men one after another
put them on and off like garments. Tell
me, is there anything more enduring than
a kingdom ? And yet, consider the palaces,
search for the royal robes. You will find
that many of these have covered the bodies
of several successive kings. And in like
manner also the crowns, and the clasps, and
the girdles—all an unstable heritage, a
property common to them all, passing over
from those who go to those who remain.
And of what worth are the possessions of
magistrates, the canopy, the silver chariot,
the golden wand ? Do not these things always attend the magistrate, yet never the
same one long, but each for a little season ?
For as the bier receives now one form, now
another, so also the insignia of office pass
from one magistrate to another. Hence,
too, the apostle has uttered very many calls

to us indicative of this thought. " For the
fashion of this world passeth away ";[1] and
the phrase, " As having nothing, and yet
possessing all things ";[2] and again, " Who
use it as not abusing it."[1]   For all these
sayings have this one intent, that it becomes us to live as creatures of a day,
awaiting the signal for our departure.

And that you may clearly see that you
are subject to the laws and ordinances of
the Lord, to which it is incumbent on you
strictly to conform, first, learn from self-
observation that both your body and soul
are wholly subject to the commands of virtue, and you are not master even of yourself, but it behooves you to act as a steward
both in word and deed, and in every movement of your life.   You have received from
the Creator a body composed of many
members and endowed with five senses for

[1] 1 Corinthians 7 : 31.   [2] 2 Corinthians 6 : 10.

the needs of life. And not even these are
free and independent, but each is subject
to law. And first, the eye is commanded,
" Look upon nature and behold what it is
right to see : the sun, illuminating all the
world ; the moon, shining upon the gloom
and dusk of night ; the stars also giving us
of themselves no great or independent
light, but reflecting the beauty they receive. Behold the earth, hairy with plants
and herbs ";[1] the sea when it lies fixed in
perfect calm, spread out like a level plain.
For the sight of these and similar things
benefit us. But other sights, which through
the eye introduce harm into the soul, shun
and flee, and put a veil over your eyes that
you may not see. For it is better to darken
the sense of sight, when it affords occasion
for " the deeds of darkness."[2] On this ac-

[1] Aristotle, De Mundo 5 : 11.
[2] Romans 13 : 12; Ephesians 5 : 11.

count, the Lord said to us through Matthew in the lesson of yesterday: " Every one that looketh on a woman to lust after her hath committed adultery with her already in his heart."[1]   And it is better to cut out the eye than that it should look upon things inordinate and lustful.[2]   And the ear also has been forbidden to listen to anything that is evil.   But it is right that it be alert to hear whatever is good, that it may transmit to the soul profitable words. But if any evil companion, ready to deal out plague and destruction approach it, and be on the point of pouring into it filth, one should flee from him as from a venomous beast.   Let the tongue also, together with the mouth, exercise discretion.   Let it say what is right; but let it refrain from forbidden things—reproaches, slanders, unjust accusation, evil speaking against the breth-

[1] Matthew 5 : 28.   [2] Matthew 18 : 9.

ren, blasphemy against God; and let it utter those things that are of good report, and
pious; let it counsel good works, and let
every man repeat the words of the sacred
Psalmist: " I said, I will set a watch over
my ways, that I sin not with my tongue:"[1]
again, " With their tongues they deal
treacherously:"[2] and again, " Why gloriest
thou in evil, O man mighty in iniquity?
All the day has thy tongue discoursed in-
justice; as a sharpened razor thou hast
wrought deceit."[3] Let the tongue taste
profitable things. Let the nose also exercise discretion, not always scenting luxury,
nor drawing into the head fragrant odors of
costly perfumes. For against such things
Isaiah vehemently inveighs.[4] Let the hand,
too, remember the commandments, that it
touch not all things indiscriminately. Let

[1] Psalm 38 : 2 (Lxx); 39: 1. [2] Psalm 5 : 10 (Lxx); 5 : 9.
[3] Psalm 51 : 3, 4 (Lxx); 52 : 1, 2.   [4] Isaiah 3: 18 ff.

it be outstretched in almsgiving, not in
plundering. Let it keep its own, not wickedly seize the things of others. Let it in
beneficent visitation touch the bodies that
are feeble and distressed, not those that are
lustful and devoted to fornication.

This discourse has shown us that we are
not our own masters, but stewards, for who-
ever is subject to laws and ordinances is a
bond-servant and subject of the lawgiver.
And if the members of our body are not
free from authority, but regulated with reference to their functions, by the will of the
Lord, what should be said to those who
think that they have, without accountabil-
ity, the possession of gold and silver and
land and all other things? O man, nothing is your own. You are a slave and
what is yours belongs to your Lord. For
a slave has no property that is really his
own.

For naked you were brought into this
life. What you have you have received by
the dispensation of your Lord; whether
you inherited it from a father, since God
has so commanded,—for parents, he says,
shall divide their possessions among their
children,[1] or have acquired affluence by
marriage,—for marriage also and the things
connected with it are ordained by God,
or by trade and agriculture and other
agencies, God cooperating in them.

You see, then, it has been made evident
that you have received things which are
not your own. Let us now further observe
what is incumbent on you, and what kind
of control you have over them. Give to
the hungry, clothe the naked, heal the
afflicted, do not neglect the needy nor the
outcast at the corners of the streets. Do
not be anxious about yourself, nor stop to

[1] Proverbs 19: 14.

consider how you will live to-morrow.[1]   If
you do these things the Scripture says that
you shall be honored by the Lawgiver.
But if you do not heed the command, you
shall be severely punished.   These things I
do not regard as characteristic of one who
is irresponsible and lives in independence.
But on the contrary, these numerous and
repeated commands suggest to me a man
strictly governed, subject to a master's laws,
and rigidly accountable for his conduct as
an administrator.   But we, living how
heedlessly, neglect the wretched and the
poor, while they die in misfortune; and
vying with each other in lavishness, spend
our money on vanities, supporting a multitude of prodigal flatterers, and trailing after
us hordes of ill-starred parasites; again,
scattering our wealth to gladiators, and for
wild beasts, and giving for horse-breeding

[1] Matthew 6: 34.

regardless of expense; and again, spending our abundance on jugglers and actors and persons equally worthless. And we have a fruitless experience, and one bordering on madness; for from expenditure that brings uncounted gain, and eternal salvation, we resolutely withhold our money, refusing to part with even a few obols; but where the expenditure is the occasion of sin and of countless pains and of the fiery punishment itself, of our own accord we let it flow. Prodigality anticipates the request, and opening all our doors, we lavish our wealth on those that are without. But this is not the mind of servants waiting for their lord, but of lusty, unbridled youths given over to revels.

But if you wish, my hearer, to see a steward administering with fear and wise discretion the things committed to him, open the book of David; find those words where one inquiring concerning the appointed time of his end, says to God, "Lord, make me to know my end, and what is the number of my days, that I may know what I lack."[1] You see in these words, as an image in a mirror, the attitude of the one who prays ; you see that he is very fearful; he foresees that which is to come, and, expecting judgment, is concerned about the appointed time, that the signal for his departure may not find him unprepared. And he seeks to number and know how many days still remain to him, in order that he may zealously fulfil his task before his Lord comes. Now if we carefully compare what the dying man experiences, and what the man who is cast out of his stewardship endures, we shall find that the end of each one of us is like that of a steward.

[1] Psalms 39:4; 38:5 (Lxx).

For the dying man turns over his control
of affairs to others, just as the steward does
his keys; the latter on being cast out of an
estate, the former on being cast out of the
world. Deeply grieved, the steward re-
tires from his own labors—from the estate
rich in vineyards, gardens, houses. What
then do you think the dying man experiences? Does he not bewail his possessions?
Does he not piteously survey his house as,
against his will, he is torn from it, and
forced in spite of his attachments, to go far
from his treasures and storehouses? And
when he comes to the appointed place,
when he hears the words, " Render the account of your stewardship, show how you
have obeyed the commandments, how you
have treated your fellow servants, whether
properly and kindly or, on the contrary,
grievously and tyrannically, smiting, punish-
ing, and withholding the alms that mercy

dictates," then if he shall be able to render
the master gracious, by showing that he
has been a faithful servant, it shall be well
with him. But if he cannot thus render
him gracious there will remain for him not
simply beating with rods, or the dark prison,
and iron fetters, but fire unquenchable and
eternal darkness, never illumined by a ray
of light, and gnashing of teeth as the Gospel has plainly taught us.[1] If indeed you
are never to be cast out of your present
possessions on the ground that they belong
to another, revel in the world and with
every sense let pleasure be unrestrained.
But if these things are to be brought to an
end and we are to enjoy them for no long
time, let us, brethren, fear our removal
hence, and live during the time of our so-
journing as the Lord has commanded. Let
us not be led away as prisoners for debt;

[1] Matthew 13:42, etc.

but let us go as free men, taking with us an approving conscience, and such an account of our conduct as will not be condemned by the Lord.

That rich man whose land brought forth abundantly, was a wicked steward of the earthly life, since in the abundance of his fruits he purposed nothing useful, but, enlarging the belly's desire and the broad and vast pockets of greed, designed all for his own enjoyment, saying, " I will pull down my barns, and build greater, and will say to myself, Thou hast much goods laid up; take thine ease, eat, drink, and be merry." [1] But while he was yet speaking, the death angel stood at his side, to conduct him from the earth. A dreadful fellow slave was come to drag him from his stewardship; and what profit was there in his plan for the gratification of his selfish desires? Now

[1] Luke 12:18, 19.

this has been vividly portrayed for our admonition.

And what does experience teach us? Do not the events of each day loudly proclaim the truth of the parable? Do we not see the man in health at midday, dead ere the appearance of the evening star? And the man strong at evening, not alive to greet the beams of dawn? And another departing this life while eating? And who is so foolish as not to perceive at a glance that daily, now one, now another, we are being removed from our stewardship here? But the good and faithful steward, whose conscience approves his own administration of his stewardship, is of Paul's opinion. For Paul, though the Lord did not urge him, was in haste to go to his Master, and longed for his release, and of his own accord resigned his stewardship, saying somewhere, "Wretched man that I am! who

shall deliver me from the body of this
death,"[1] and again, " But for me it is well
to depart and be with Christ."[2]   But one
who is earthly in mind, and really akin to
the clods, being confounded at the change
which overtakes him, utters such lamentations as did the man of the parable;
" What shall I do, because my Lord takes
away the stewardship from me?   I cannot
dig, to beg I am ashamed."   The lamenta-
tion of an idle and pleasure-loving man!
For to weep at his departure, and to lament
the sensuous enjoyments of the flesh, is
proof that one is engrossed in his estate;
and to be incapable of toil is the mark of an
idle and supine life.   For if he had been
accustomed to industry, he would not have
hesitated to dig.

But further, to carry out the meaning of
the parable, after removal to the eternal

[1] Romans 7 : 24.   [2] Philippians 1 : 23.

world there is no longer place for impor-
tunity. And therefore let no one of them
there say, " I cannot dig." For even if he
could, no one would give him the oppor-
tunity. To this life belongs the obedience
of the commandments, and to the life to
come the reward. So that if you have
done nothing here, it will be useless for
you to think of digging, since you will
have left the vines behind. Nor will you
benefit yourself at all by entreating. And
we have a notable example of this in the
story of the foolish virgins, who were
delayed for lack of oil, and shamelessly
asked it from those who were wise.[1] But
they got no help, and turned away unsuc-
cessful; the narrative showing that, at the
bridegroom's appearing, no one may use
another's oil, that is, another's rectitude,
for his own benefit. For each one is

[1] Matthew 25 : 1ff.

clothed with his own conduct as with a
garment, whether it be splendid and costly,
or mean and like a beggar's cloak.   But to
put off this garment is not possible, nor to
remove it and exchange it for another, nor
to beautify and adorn it by the gift or loan
of another in the time of judgment, but
each one remains such as he is in truth,
whether poor in good deeds or rich.

But what can we say concerning the re-
mission of debts which the unjust steward
contrived, that he might through his fellow
servants secure relief for himself from the
hardships of his downfall?   For it is not
easy to convert this into allegory consonant
with Scripture, but after long reflection
something like this occurred to me: All
of us who busy ourselves about the rest to
which we are destined, by giving what is
another's, work to our own advantage;
now by what is another's I mean what

belongs to the Lord. For nothing is our
own, but all things belong to him.   When,
therefore, any one anticipating his end and
his removal to the next world, lightens the
burden of his sins by good deeds, either by
canceling the obligations of debtors, or by
supplying the poor with abundance, by
giving what belongs to the Lord, he gains
many friends, who will attest his goodness
before the Judge, and secure him by their
testimony a place of happiness.   Now they
are called witnesses, who have secured for
their benefactors favor from the Judge, not
because they inform him of anything, as
though he were ignorant, or did not know,
but in the sense that what has been done
for them relieves those who have helped
them from the punishment of their sins.
For just as the blood of Abel was said to
cry unto God,[1] in like manner the good

[1] Genesis 4: 10.

deed, too, shall be said to testify on behalf of the upright in our Lord, Christ Jesus. Now to him be glory forever and ever. Amen.

III

AGAINST COVETOUSNESS

Texts Quoted by Asterius in the Body of his Discourse

No servant can serve two masters: for either he will hate the one, and love the other; or else he will hold to the one, and despise the other. Ye cannot serve God and mammon.—*Luke 16 · 13.*

For this ye know, that no whoremonger, nor unclean person, nor covetous man, who is an idolater, hath any inheritance in the kingdom of Christ and of God.—*Eph. 5 : 5.*

For the love of money is the root of all evil: which while some coveted after, they have erred from the faith, and pierced themselves through with many sorrows.—*1 Tim. 6 : 10.*

And he said unto them, Take heed, and beware of covetousness: for a man's life consisteth not in the abundance of the things which he possesseth.

And he spake a parable unto them, saying, The ground of a certain rich man brought forth plentifully:

And he thought within himself, saying, What shall I do, because I have no room where to bestow my fruits?

And he said, This will I do: I will pull down my barns, and build greater; and there will I bestow all my fruits and my goods.

And I will say to my soul, Soul, thou hast much goods laid up for many years; take thine ease, eat, drink, and be merry.

But God said unto him, Thou fool, this night thy soul shall be required of thee: then whose shall those things be, which thou hast provided?

So is he that layeth up treasure for himself, and is not rich toward God.—*Luke 12 : 15-21.*

III

AGAINST COVETOUSNESS

CHRISTIANS and sharers of a heav-
enly calling,[1] you country folk, and
all who come from the towns, you who in
concord have gathered at the present feast,
—for by a general address I embrace you
all,—has each one of you thoughtfully considered and realized why we are assembled?
And why are martyrs honored by the con-
struction of notable buildings and by these
annual assemblies, and what end did our
fathers have in view when they ordained
the things we see, and left the established
custom to their descendants? Is it not evident to one who concentrates his thought

[1] Hebrews 3 : 1.

on this subject even for a short time, that
these things have been given permanent
form to rouse us to pious emulation, and
that the feasts constitute public schools for
our souls, in order that while we honor the
martyrs, we may learn to imitate their
sturdy piety; that lending the ear to the
gathered teachers, we may learn some useful thing which we did not know before,—
either the certainty of some doctrine, or
the explanation of some difficult Scripture,
—or may hear some discourse that will improve our morals?

But you seem to me to have abandoned
your care for virtue, to have forgotten your
zeal on behalf of your souls, and to have
devoted all your thought to the rubbish of
mammon and the business of the markets;
some bargaining yourselves; some greedily
haggling with competing dealers in order
to reduce their prices. But transfer your

love to the church. Abandon the love
of money, that mad passion of the market.
Turn from it as from a disorderly courtezan
who, embellished with foreign stuffs and with
the brilliant colors of the apothecary, smiles
upon the multitude. Love the church, divine and discreet, modestly attired, with look
august and grave. For thus Solomon says
in the book of Proverbs, "Forsake her not,
and she shall preserve thee: love her, and
she shall keep thee."[1] Do not pass her by
with contempt, nor deem the things that
lie near us on this table[2] of little worth because it is possible for you to procure them
freely. But desire them all the more because we do not sit, as hucksters, with bal-
ance and scales; but seek only one gain,—
the salvation of the hearer.

There has been read to us from the Acts

[1] Proverbs 4 : 6 (Lxx).
[2] Probably the Scriptures were on the table.

the speech of Paul to Festus and Agrippa,
—Paul the faithful apostle and wise speaker.[1]
You doubtless saw, my hearer, if you gave
heed, how he boldly declares the truth, but,
mingling deference to Agrippa with his
boldness, he softens the harsh tribunal to
gentleness, subduing them by the manner
of his speech, as wild beasts by song.
Zechariah, too, has prophesied to-day,
opening to us the door of the great mysteries of the Only-begotten, by the stone
with the seven quick-glancing eyes, and by
the golden candlestick with its seven lamps,
and the trunks of the two olive trees.[2]
There are many kindred Scriptures full of
profit for us, into all of which I wished to
go that I might show you the abundance
of the spiritual feast. But I must fulfil the
promise that I made yesterday. For after
we had brought many accusations against

[1] Acts 26.   [2] Zechariah 3 : 9; 4 : 14.

covetousness, but had scarcely laid bare its vanity, we deferred until to-day the proof of the charges. Listen, therefore, and show yourselves wise judges of the truth; for your decision affects your own salvation, not that of others; and each of you casts his vote of condemnation against his own soul, as though driving it out of house or town.

Covetousness, then, is not simply being mad for money, and other possessions, wishing to add to what you have that to which you have no right, but, to speak more broadly, it is the desire to have in every transaction more than is due or belongs to you. And you know that the devil was the first to have this fault; for he was an archangel, and appointed to the most honorable life and station; but the arrogant creature conceived of absolute rule, and rebellion against God, and was

thereafter cast down from heaven, and, falling into this atmosphere of earth, he became your malicious neighbor. So he did
not attain the divinity to which he aspired,
and he lost the rank which he had enjoyed
of being archangel; an unfaithful servant,
changed by gradually increasing audacity
into a robber ;—the dog of the Greek fable,
who was both deprived of his meat and
failed to grasp the shadow—for how could
he grasp an intangible thing?

After him, the first man was beguiled
into the love of pleasure, and by eating the
forbidden fruit lost immortality,[1] as Esau
afterward lost his birthright for a dish of
pottage.[2] And love of more introduced
into our life these languages of ours, the
many tongues of men.[3] For men who
through plenty had become wanton, think-

[1] Genesis 3: 3.   [3] Genesis 11 : 1–9.
[2] Genesis 25 : 29–34.

ing that the heavens were accessible to them, foolishly made a preposterous tower for mounting up to the sky, and so caused mankind, which had been of one language, to speak with different tongues; in seeking more than they had, they themselves were not only confounded but left to mankind the weariness of hearing unintelligible tongues, and of searching for their interpretation.

And what of Pharaoh? How came he to fall into difficulties and to be afflicted with plagues? Was it not through covetousness, through the desire of being lord over a strange people which by no means belonged to his kingdom? And, since he did not let those go who belonged to another, he lost those who were his own; some in the smiting of the first-born and others in the pursuit through the sea. For I do not mention the rivers flowing blood, and the infinite generation of frogs, and the destruction wrought by locusts, and the eruption of boils, and the death of four-footed beasts, and all the evil to which Egypt was condemned on account of her ruler's covetousness.[1]

Again, somewhere else I have learned the outcome of this sin, how leprosy in a moment spread over the body of the covetous. Recall with me, if you are historically inclined, and fond of hearing of Elisha's deeds, how Naaman the Syrian bathed in the Jordan, and was healed of his leprosy, and how his malady passed over upon Gehazi, the prophet's servant, a covetous and foolish young man, who received raiment and silver for his master's free act of healing.[2] How did Absalom, that fiery and impetuous young man, son of an indulgent father, become a parricide? Was

[1] Exodus 8-14.   [2] 2 Kings 5.

it not by prematurely seeking the inheritance of the kingdom and leaping like a
robber upon what was another's?[1] And
Judas, also,—what drove him out from the
company of the apostles, and made him
a traitor instead of an apostle? Was it
not the treasury at first dishonestly admin-
istered, and then the getting of the shameful price?[2] Why does the Acts of the
Apostles tell in tragic vein of Ananias and
Sapphira? Is it not because they were
thieves of what was their own, and viola-
tors of their own offerings?[3] The day will
soon fail me if I try to enumerate the servants of covetousness.

But now, leaving ancient history, let us
interrogate the experience of daily life, and
learn what sort of a creature it recognizes
in covetousness, and how hard it is to get

[1] 2 Samuel 15. [2] Acts 5 : 1-10.
[3] John 12 : 6; Matthew 26 : 15.

rid of; for whomsoever it seizes, ever waxing but never waning, it grows old with its victims and abides with them to the end.

The lustful and the lover of his body, even if he be for a long time mad in his desires, when he becomes old, or sees the object of his affection, his body, now aged and the bloom departed, finds that there is a limit to his disorder. The glutton himself withdraws from his indulgence when surfeited, or when his digestive organs become weak, and their intense desire for food is gone. The ambitious man after having attained great notoriety ceases to desire to show himself off. But the disease of covetousness is an evil hard to rid one's self of. And just as this ivy, the plant flourishing and ever green, creeping up the trees that grow near, coils tight about the trunks wherever it touches—and even if they suffer harm or wither, it does not die, unless some one with an axe severs its serpent-like coils—so it is not easy to free the soul from covetousness, whether the body be youthful or beginning to grow old, unless some sober consideration enter in and like a knife cut off the disease.

The covetous man is odious to the members of his household, severe to his domestics, useless to his friends, ungracious to strangers, troublesome to his neighbors, a sorry companion to his wife, a penurious rearer of children, a bad master of himself; at night full of anxiety, by day absorbed, talking to himself like one demented; abounding in wealth, yet groaning as though in need; not enjoying what he has, and yet seeking what he has not; not using his own, yet casting avaricious eyes upon the property of others. Such a man has a great flock of sheep that fills the folds in which it is penned, and covers the plains

on which it pastures. And if a single
sheep belonging to his neighbor appear in
good flesh, taking no notice of his own
vast flock he lays greedy siege to that *one*
sheep of his neighbor. The same is true
in the case of his kine and of his horses;
nor is it otherwise in the matter of his land.
The house is crowded with everything, but
nothing is made any use of. For it is impossible for a greedy person to have any
enjoyment, but his house is almost like a
grave. For see, graves are often full of
silver and gold, but no one uses the riches.
The body is not sustained by them; the
soul finds no satisfaction in them; for alms
are not scattered by the right hand of the
dead.

Now let some one who has been seized
with this disease of covetousness tell me
what is the object of this toil for gain?
For I know that many with whom I am

acquainted, love money more when they
are sick than when they are in health.   If
the doctor prescribes for their recovery
some inexpensive medicine, such as parsley
or thyme or anise, which can be procured
without expense, they readily heed his di-
rections.   But if he mentions some drug,
the ingredients of which are rich and com-
plex, and they are sent to the apothecary
or the perfumer to purchase it, they give
up their lives rather than open their purses.
For being earthly-minded they think the
possession of earthly things to be life itself.
These men are profoundly depressed by
general prosperity and delighted by general distress.   They pray that intolerable
burdens of taxation may be imposed by
public proclamation that they may increase
their money by usury.   They want to see
their neighbors throttled by money-lenders,
in order that they may secure for them-

selves their farms, their chattels, or live
stock, when through necessity they are
thrown on the market at a low price. And
they keep continually looking up at the
sky, like those philosophers whose work it
is to investigate astronomical phenomena,
not studying the movement of a star, nor
trying to observe what house is occupied
by one of the planets,[1] but curious about
the state of the atmosphere, whether the
signs that present themselves promise a
downfall of rain or a drought. And if they
see any portent of any calamity threatening to fall on the community at large, they
rejoice over it. They gather everything
into their warehouses, which they closely
seal and secure with double bars, while they
continually measure and reckon up their
stores. And while the covetous man cher-

[1] They believed that each planet had its own house
in the heavens. Cf. Century Dict, " House," sec. 10.

ishes such expectation and in his mind's eye sees himself rich, if a thick cloud arise, he is frightened as though danger were imminent. If showers besprinkle the earth he begins to weep. And if there comes rain enough to mitigate the drought, it makes him perfectly miserable. Thereafter in all he does he goes about cogitating on the grain, as on a son in peril, thinking by what means, by what device it may be preserved for a long time, and escape danger by insects. But when he sees that the weather is dry, as physicians treat persons wasting away by perspiration, spreading out his grain he stirs and freshens it, toilsomely tends it, devises a shelter against the noonday heat, and strips off the screens at night, that it may be fanned by the night winds.

To him, engaged in this distressful toil, the poor man presents himself, asking for some of the endangered grain, but he does not give it; or, if he gives it, he bestows it parsimoniously, and half-heartedly, parting with it with extreme reluctance. Therefore, I beseech you, if you are such a man, do not undergo these infinite hardships. For the covetous man who lives in luxury is deserving of pity, since he bounds his existence with the belly's enjoyment and other pleasures, regarding this as the goal of humanity. But in the case of the mean and penurious, his wretchedness has no limit, since he receives the goods of many, and does not give even to himself, and so has nothing for his pains. For who does not know that nothing, except the virtues, exists for its own sake, but we do one thing in order that we may accomplish another? No sailor traverses the sea simply for the sake of sailing, and no farmer passes his life in toil simply for the sake of farming; but it is manifest that both persevere amid their hardships that they may secure, the one the increase of the earth, and the other the wealth of maritime trade. But tell me now, O covetous man, what is your goal? To accumulate? And what kind of an object in life is this, to heap up and gloat over unused substance? The very sight, he replies, delights me. Then attack your disorder in another way. For you can allay this longing with what belongs to others. If the glitter of silver delights you, sit beside the silversmiths and gaze steadfastly upon the strong and glittering sheen ; or haunt the markets, and enjoy the richly wrought vessels, platters and pitchers. For the sight of them is free and unhindered. Watch the money-changers also who are continually reckoning and counting the coin at their tables; but, better yet, yield to good advice and give up this inclination. For amendment is easy, since covetousness is not a necessity of nature, but a direction of choice, and to change it is not difficult for those who consider their own advantage.

Pass over in thought to the time to come, when you shall be no more; when a small plot of earth shall hold your body, insensate, returned to dust, and a little tablet, a few spans in size, shall cover all that remains. Where then will be your wealth and your gathered treasures? Who will be the heir of what you leave behind? For it is by no means certain that it will be he whom you suppose. If you leave children, perhaps they will be beaten, and driven weeping from their ancestral home by some covetous man like you. But if, being childless, you mean to transmit the inheritance to one of your friends, do not regard your will as an immutable law, a thing strong and incapable of being set aside. It will require but little exertion to make the writing invalid. Do you not see those who are constantly contesting wills in the courts, how by all kinds of attacks they wrest them by putting forward as advocates skilful lawyers, invoking the aid of eloquent orators, suborning witnesses, corrupting judges? So from what you see while you are alive, learn what will happen after you are dead. If you have gotten your wealth justly, use it, as did the blessed Job, for needful purposes; if unjustly, restore it to those who have been defrauded of it, as you would a thing captured in war, giving back either just what you took, or that with something added, as did Zacchæus.[1] If you have no wealth, do not get any by wickedness. For as you go the inevitable way, your sin, a bitter portion, will

[1] Luke 19:8.

follow you, while the enjoyment of your ill-gotten gains will be left behind for whom you know not. And then you will admire David because he says, " He heap- eth up riches, and knoweth not who shall gather them."[1] And observe also the rich man contrasted with Lazarus, of whom we have just read in the Gospels,—a narrative which is no fable composed to inspire terror, but a true picture transmitted to us of what is to be.

The fine linen perished, the kingdom departed to another, the luxuries passed away; but the sin of them went with him, as a person's shadow follows him when walking. And for this reason, after his extravagant banquets, and his luxurious table, he begs for a drop of water that falls from a leper's finger, and calls to alleviate his punishment the beggar who, perhaps,

[1] Psalms 39:6; 38:7 (Lxx).

when he lay at the gate, did not even have
hands; for surely if he had had them he
would have driven away the dogs that
licked his sores. And he desires to join
Lazarus, seeing him on the other side, and
is hindered by the ditch or gulf between
them, which was no hole that had been
digged nor artificial ditch like that which
one can see between hostile camps in war.
But the Scripture, I think, means that his
sins were the obstacle that cut off the approach of the condemned to the righteous.
And the prophet Isaiah sets his seal to my
interpretation, when he sternly rebukes a
foolish people and says, " Is the Lord's
hand shortened, that it cannot save? Or
is his ear heavy, that it cannot hear? But
your sins stand between you and God."[1]
But if sin is able to separate men from
God, nothing can be more sinful than covet-

[1] Isaiah 59: 1, 2 (Lxx).

ousness, which Paul, the herald of the truth, truly calls idolatry, and the root and parent of all evils.

For how are those drawn into the service of demons who were once of the company of Christians and partakers in the mysteries? Is it not by the desire of acquiring great wealth, and of becoming masters of what belongs to others? Upon receiving from godless and impious men promises either of official preferment or of wealth from royal treasuries, they quickly put off their religion as a garment. And such examples occurring in previous times, memory and tradition have preserved and handed down to us. And there are also instances which belong to our own generation, and are within the range of our experience. For when that emperor[1] who all at once cast aside the character of a Christian, and

[1] The Emperor Julian.

disclosed the farce he had long been acting, himself shamelessly sacrificed to demons, and offered many gifts to those who were willing to do the same, how many left the church and ran to pagan altars! How many, taking the bait of emolument, swallowed with it the hook of apostasy, and branded with disgrace are wandering about among the towns, objects of hatred; pointed at as betrayers of Christ, for the sake of a little money; stricken from the list of Christians, as was Judas from the roll of the apostles; known by the name of apostate, as horses are known by the marks branded upon them; who simply allowed themselves to be drawn into the basest of all sins, and promptly followed the teacher of unhallowed and abominable impiety!

Thus, therefore, as the apostle says, covetousness is idolatry also,[1] and is the root

[1] Ephesians 5 : 5.

of all evils,[1] generating untold iniquities.
For as those who seek gold in the bowels
of the earth say that the gold-bearing rock
lies in great quantities at its very source
and the place of its origin, and thence in
veins, one running this way and another
that, extends to a great distance, and is
prolonged in many ramifications, somewhat
as the roots of trees diverge from the trunk,
so here, while I see many offshoots, I find
them all bound together in one root, covetousness.   Indeed, with no impropriety does
a sermon against covetousness draw its illustration from gold.   For gold I see the parricide taking violent steps against his father's
life, reverencing neither the hoary head,
nor the paternal dignity, but vexed at the
lengthening life of the old man.   For seeing everything abundant at home, yet having no authority over what he sees, he longs

[1] 1 Timothy 6: 10.

to be master of this paternal wealth, and
finds his father's authority irksome. At
first he keeps silent, and represses the
malady of covetousness in the depths of
his soul; but after his desire has increased
with time, and his soul is filled with it, all
at once he lets the wickedness break forth,
as waters break through their embankments.
And thereafter he behaves insufferably to
his father, all but driving him to the grave,
while he is still alive and well. If he mounts
his horse with agility, the son is astounded;
if he eats heartily, his son murmurs. If he
early arouses the servants to their duties,
the son is grieved by the alertness and
vigor of the old man. But if he gives
away any of his property, or releases a
servant from bondage, then indeed as silly
and half-witted and living beyond the proper
limits of life, and as a squanderer of what
belongs to another, he must listen to every

impious reproach, and be blackguarded like a drunkard, and upbraided for not dying soon enough.

This is your fruit, O abominable covetousness! Spurred on by you, the child becomes his parent's enemy. You fill the earth with robbers and murderers, and the sea with pirates, cities with tumult, courts with false witnesses, false accusers, betrayers, advocates, and judges who incline whichever way you draw them. Covetousness is the mother of inequality, unmerciful, hating mankind, most cruel. On account of it, the life of men is full of inequality. Some being surfeited, loathe the abundance of their possessions, as one disgorges food which has been too greedily swallowed; while others are in peril through extreme hunger and want. Some lie down under gilded roofs and live in houses that are like small cities, adorned

with sumptuous baths and chambers, and
most extensive porches, and every kind of
extravagance, while others have not the
shelter of two boards. When they cannot
live in open air, they either take refuge beside the furnaces of the baths, or, finding
the attendants of the baths inhospitable,
they dig into the dung like swine, and so
contrive to get for themselves the needful
warmth. Such is the marked disparity in
the conditions of life, between men created
equal in worth, and the cause of this disordered and anomalous state of things is
nothing else than covetousness. One is
put to shame by his naked limbs; the
other, beside having almost countless garments, dresses his walls with purple hang-
ings. The poor man has not on his
wooden table any bread to break; while
the luxurious man sitting at his broad silver
table is delighted with its glitter. How

much more just it would be that the poor
man should feast to the full on the other's
luxury, and that the support of the needy
should be the decoration of the rich man's
table! One man, aged and unable to walk,
or lame by reason of some outrageous
mutilation, does not possess the ass that he
needs to carry him about, while another
does not know his droves of horses for
their very multitude. One lacks oil to
light his lamps, while another has a fortune simply in lamp-stands. One has only
the ground for his bed, while he who is
unreasonably rich. is dazzled by the
splendor of his couch, with its silver balls
and chains instead of cords. These are
the results of insatiable covetousness. For
had it not introduced inequality into life,
these anomalous heights and depths would
not have existed, nor would manifold misfortunes have made our life joyless and tearful.

On account of covetousness men lose
their natural friendship for one another,
and whet their swords and array themselves
against each other and like wild beasts
fight one another with great ferocity.   But
how can one relate the consequences of
these things?   Massive walls are thrown
down by engines, cities are taken, women
led captives, and children enslaved.   The
land is wasted and ravaged, and the trees
are warred against as though they were
wrong-doers.   There is great slaughter of
those who are in the prime of life, and
torrents of blood stream from the wretched
corpses ; and the wealth of the conquered
is the victors' prize.   There are, moreover,
the lamentations of widows, the tears of
orphans, who bewail at once both their fathers and their freedom.   He who was day
before yesterday possessor of great wealth,
stretches forth his right hand to beg a bit

of bread, and he who had many slaves at
the loom, and houses full of garments, now
clothed in rags does the work of a slave,
forced to carry water and scrape the dung
from the stable, and to perform most
menial duties. There are besides countless
evils which it is impossible to compass all
at once. But of all of these, the beginning
and cause and root is greed, unrighteous
love of the goods that belong to another.
And if any one should extirpate this
passion from the human heart, profound
peace would be inevitably introduced into
our life, and wars and tumults would be
banished from among men, and all would
return to the natural condition of love and
friendliness. On this account, our Lord
also carefully heals this disease, once declaring in his teachings; " Ye cannot serve
God and mammon;" [1] and on another oc-

[1] Luke 16: 13.

casion declaring wretched the rich man
who was just about to die, even as he was
picturing to himself the protracted enjoyment of luxury;[1] and elsewhere teaching
that that man was perfect who divided all
that he had among the needy, and went
over to a self-denying life, which is the
mother and companion of virtue.[2]

But I seem to hear, even though they
are silent, those who are wont to say
such things as these to their teachers:
"How shall we continue to live, if we do
not care for the getting of money? and
how shall we satisfy our needs? How are
loans to be repaid, and how shall a gift be
bestowed upon him who asks it, if we are
all to follow your admonition and be
poor?" This is the objection of an unbe-
liever, the speech of one devoid of un-
derstanding, who does not know that God

[1] Luke 12: 20.   [2] Matthew 19: 21.

is our Master, the director of our life,
and that he himself furnishes the living
creature what it needs, the means of getting both necessary food and needful
clothing. For the providence of God is
over all his works, and the misfortune of
poverty never overtakes one who is rich in
faith. By presenting one of the divine
narratives in proof of what I now affirm I
shall, I think, offer sufficient evidence of it.

In the history of the kings a widow
woman is mentioned who, on account of
her solitary condition was greatly op-
pressed.[1] A greedy and churlish creditor
pestered her, threatening to take away as
pledges for her debts, her sons who were
all she had left. And when the crisis in
her affairs came and none of the rich had
pity on her, she went to him who had humanity and faith. Now this was Elisha the

[1] 2 Kings 4: 1-7.

prophet, a man poor in this world's goods, but abounding in immaterial wealth; an unworldly soul from among the plowmen, houseless, homeless, clad with but one garment; who had just had a legacy, and had received as his inheritance a cheap sheepskin and an invisible blessing, which fell from the chariot of fire.[1] Yet he did not send away the suppliant disappointed, nor did he despair of helping her because he had not what she asked, nor did he utter any sordid and doubting words, as many would have done, such as, "And where am I to get money to pay your debt?" but, like a most excellent physician when there are no medicines to be had, by an unexpected device he found a remedy for the disease and said, "Woman, what have you in the house?[2] Call to mind whether you have anything within, however small. For

[1] 2 Kings 2: 9–13.   [2] 2 Kings 4: 2.

no one is so poor as to have absolutely
nothing." And when she replied that she
had a cruse with a little oil remaining in it,
he said, " Prepare me a multitude of vessels." So she got them ready and filled
them from the cruse. Thus the debt
was paid to the money-lender, and the
woman departed, having found a way out
of her difficulties. For the very little oil
which she had told the prophet she pos-
sessed, contrary to her expectation gushed
forth and filled all the jars she had made
ready, and it ceased to flow only when
there was not another vessel to receive it.
And the gift was commensurate with her
need. That was indeed oil which no plant,
but the mercies of God, produced. Buy
yourselves this knowledge, if you can, you
kings, rulers, men of wealth, from the rising to the setting sun. You who are rich

in worldly wisdom, get the gift of the
plowman prophet, which could not be
taken away from him who had received it.
For the possessions which you so eagerly
desire are beset with countless risks ; thieves
who break into houses, tyrants who confis-
cate, flatterers who plot, the sea that over-
whelms, and the earth that quakes and
yawns. Therefore let the right hand of
God be the hope and treasury of men,—
the hand that led his people out of Egypt,[1]
and in the desert provided abundance of
good things,[2] which brought Habakkuk to
Daniel,[3] and preserved Ishmael when he
had been cast down from his mother's
arms ;[4] which provides for those of every
generation ; and which, finally, multiplied

---

[1] Exodus 14.   [2] Exodus 16; Numbers 11.

[3] In the history of Bel and the Dragon, Habakkuk
is said to have carried food to Daniel in the den of
lions at Babylon.

[4] Genesis 21 : 15-19.

five barley loaves so that they equaled a great harvest, and one loaf supplied a thousand hungry men and filled a basket with fragments besides.[1]

Now to our God be glory forever and ever. Amen.

[1] John 6 : 9–13.

IV

ON THE FESTIVAL OF THE CALENDS

The preacher had no text. His sermon is an earnest protest against the evils into which New Year's festivals had drifted in his day. This is the earliest extant New Year's sermon, and in that respect it is unique. The strange customs portrayed in it make it peculiarly fascinating.

IV

ON THE FESTIVAL OF THE CALENDS

YESTERDAY and to-day two feasts, not only unrelated and discordant, but wholly adverse and hostile to each other, have been celebrated. One is of the rabble without, gathering, in large sums, the money of mammon, and bringing in its train bargaining, vulgar and mean. The other is of holy and true religion, inculcating acquaintance with God, and the virtue of the purified life. And since many, preferring the luxury and absorption which arise from vanity, have left off going to church, come, let us with a discourse dispel from your souls this foolish and harmful delight, which as a sort of inflammation of the brain, with laughter and jesting, induces death. And in the treatment of the subject I may fittingly emulate Solomon. For in counseling young men to keep themselves from the snares of licentiousness, in order to make his own admonition cogent and effective, he personifies excess as an abandoned woman, and, by portraying all her wickedness, he thus exposes her to her dupes as deserving of their hatred.[1] Wherefore I, too, after showing the vanity of the human heart in my discourse, will attempt to convert the lovers of pleasure from their misdirected zeal.

Of a public feast, this, then, should be the rule and law: first, that the festival have a distinct object; and then that the mirth be common to all; not that a part enjoy themselves and the rest be left in dejection and

[1] Proverbs 5 : 3–6.

pain. For this latter condition is characteristic of war rather than of a feast, since it is
inevitable that the victors parade in their
victory, while the conquered bewail their
misfortune. Now in these days, first, it is
not clear for what object this festival is celebrated. For the many legends current concerning it are mutually subversive and dis-
close nothing certain. Then I see only a
few making merry, while the mass of the
people are melancholy, even though they
try to conceal their dejection by a cheerful
demeanor; while all is noise and tumult,
the multitude heedlessly jostling one another.

It is a recollection of, and a rejoicing
over, the new year. What kind of rejoicing, sir? First, then, I observe the manner of meeting, of what a sort it is, and
how suspicious and unfriendly! With a
voice feeble and faint the salutation drops

from the lips. Then follows the kiss, as a prelude to the New Year's present. The mouth indeed is kissed, but it is the coin that is loved,—the form of a sale and the deed of covetousness! But where there is pure and frank friendship, kindnesses are freely bestowed with no expectation of gain. So, while on this New Year's festival many things are carried about everywhere, and money is given, there is no pretext of legitimate barter, nor does any one claim it. It is not a wedding, so that one might call it the prodigality of a haughty bridegroom. Nor am I able to call the expenditure almsgiving, since no poor man is relieved of his misfortune. One cannot call what takes place exchange, for the multitude exchange nothing with one another. But to call it a free gift is still more inappropriate, since the giving is by necessity. What, then, are we to call the festival, or the money spent in it? I cannot make out. But tell me, you who have been wearing yourselves out in preparing for it. Give an account of it, as we do of the festivals which are genuine and according to the will of God. We celebrate the birth of Christ, since at this time God manifested himself in the flesh. We celebrate the Feast of Lights (Epiphany), since by the forgiveness of our sins we are led forth from the dark prison of our former life into a life of light and uprightness. Again, on the day of the resurrection we adorn ourselves and march through the streets with joy, because that day reveals to us immortality and the transformation into a higher existence. Thus we keep these feasts and the rest of them in orderly succession. For every human event there is a reason, but that which lacks reasonable explanation and purpose is stuff and nonsense.

Oh, the absurdity of it! All stalk about open-mouthed, hoping to receive something from one another. Those who have given are dejected; those who have received a gift do not retain it, for the present is handed on from one to another, and he who received it from an inferior gives it to a superior. The money of this festival is as unstable as the ball of boys at play, for it is passed quickly on from me to my neighbor. It is but a new form of bribery and servility, having inevitably linked with it the element of necessity. For the more eminent and respectable man shames one into giving. A person of lower rank asks outright, and it all moves by degrees toward the pockets of the most eminent men. And you may see just such a thing as happens in the confluence of waters. There a streamlet melts into and mingles its waters with one larger than itself, and it in turn

loses itself in one still more copious, and
many small streams joined together become
part of the neighboring river; this again,
of another greater still, and so on, one join-
ing another, until the last one brings the
waters to rest in the depth and breadth of
the sea.

This is misnamed a feast, being full of
annoyance; since going out-of-doors is
burdensome, and staying within doors is not
undisturbed. For the common vagrants
and the jugglers of the stage, dividing themselves into squads and hordes, hang about
every house. The gates of public officials
they besiege with especial persistence, actu-
ally shouting and clapping their hands until
he that is beleaguered within, exhausted,
throws out to them whatever money he has
and even what is not his own. And these
mendicants going from door to door follow
one after another, and, until late in the

evening, there is no relief from this nuisance. For crowd succeeds crowd, and shout, shout, and loss, loss.

Such is this delectable feast, the source of debt and usury, the occasion of poverty, the beginning of misfortunes. And if a man become prosperous by honest industry, incredible as that may seem, and not by the craft of the usurer, even he is dragged along as one who has failed to pay the royal taxes; he weeps like one whose goods are confiscated, and he laments like a man who falls among thieves. He is dogged, he is flogged, and if there be in the house any little thing for the support of his wife and wretched children, this he lets go, and sits him down hungry with his whole family on this glorious feast-day. A new law this, of evil custom, that annoyance be celebrated as a feast, and man's want be called a festival!

This festival teaches even the little children, artless and simple, to be greedy, and accustoms them to go from house to house and to offer novel gifts, fruits covered with silver tinsel. For these they receive in return gifts double their value, and thus the tender minds of the young begin to be impressed with that which is commercial and sordid.

But as to the sturdy and honest farmers! What things this feast-day brings to them! It renders the city a place to be shunned rather than visited, and they fly from it more timidly than hares from nets. Such as are found within it are flogged, treated with drunken violence, what they have in their hands is snatched from them; they are warred upon in time of peace, are jeered at, and mocked with words and deeds. Even our most excellent and guileless prophets, the unmistakable representa-

tives of God, who when unhindered in their
work are our faithful ministers, are treated
with insolence.   Thus it is, then, with those
in office, thus with the poor, thus with the
children, thus with the rustics.   For some
are distressed, some murmur, and some
learn what it were better not to know.

And let us consider how the soldiers under arms, too, are benefited by this feast.
As to money they are losers.   They offer
their entire wages as pay for one debauch.
As to manners and habits they are made
worse.   For they learn vulgarity, and the
practices of actors.   Their military disci-
pline is relaxed and slackened.   They make
sport of the laws and the government of
which they have been appointed guardians.
For they ridicule and insult the august government.   They mount a chariot as though
upon a stage; they appoint pretended lic-
tors and publicly act like buffoons.   This is

the nobler part of their ribaldry. But their
other doings, how can one mention them?
Does not the champion, the lion-hearted
man, the man who when armed is the admiration of his friends and the terror of his
foes, loose his tunic to his ankles, twine a
girdle about his breast, use a woman's
sandal, put a roll of hair on his head in
feminine fashion, and ply the distaff full of
wool, and with that right hand which once
bore the trophy, draw out the thread, and
changing the tone of his voice utter his
words in the sharper feminine treble?
These are the good uses of the festival,
these the advantages of to-day's public
feast !

Even the eminent consuls who have attained the pinnacle of human rewards,
spend their money in vanity, scattering
large sums for no righteous end, but for the
fruit of sin. Their folly is as conspicuous

as their throne is high. For being seated
on many human thrones, and administering the greatest offices of the kingdom,
they take unsparingly from every source
the largest possible amounts, some appro-
priating the provision money of poor soldiers, others oftentimes selling justice and
truth, and others extracting untold wealth
from royal coffers and greedily gathering
together money from all quarters, disdain-
ing no source of income, however unbe-
coming or unjust. They provoke God:
now presiding in public, and, a little later,
lavishing their gold upon charioteers, ill-
starred flute-players, buffoons, dancers, the
effeminate and harlots, who offer their persons for sale to the public. Moreover, they
squander their gold upon the beast-fighters,
blood-stained and desperate, and even upon
the beasts themselves. For it is manifest
that their gold supports the wild beasts, too,

buying flesh for some, grain for others. And all this money is prodigally spent for one object, that their names may be written upon contracts.[1] What folly! What blindness! God promises to write the names of those who feed the poor in living books, immortal, incorruptible, which moth does not consume, nor time destroy. For these inscriptions you do not care. Do you take no account of the blessed promise, nor seek to be written in the remembrance of God? For this is the Book that abides. But you count it of great importance to have your names written down by the notaries, to be mentioned by those who buy slaves, and to be applauded by vulgar flatterers. You thus show yourselves poor judges of what is truly useful and advantageous. Give to

[1] In the Byzantine period contracts were usually dated by the names of the ruling consuls, who thus became the eponyms of the year.

the crippled beggar, and not to the dissolute
musician. Give to the widow instead of
the harlot; instead of to the woman of the
street, to her who is piously secluded.
Lavish your gifts upon the holy virgins
singing psalms unto God, and hold the
shameless psaltery in abhorrence, which by
its music catches the licentious before it is
seen. Satisfy the orphan, pay the poor
man's debt, and you shall have a glory
that is eternal. You empty a multitude of
purses for shameful pastime, and ribald
laughter, not knowing how many poor
men's tears you are giving, from whom˙
your wealth has been gathered; how many
have been imprisoned, how many beaten,
how many have come near death by the
halter, to furnish what dancers to-day receive. And what is the end? Vanity.
After it all, a little grave, a garment worth
a few obols, shrouding the poor body.

After a little, forgetfulness,—the inevitable experience of time, veiling all the things striven for. After that, the judgment of God and the inexorable punishment of evil choice.

Where now are the consuls? Consider those of very recent times. Was not one caught in the sudden uprising of an armed multitude and did he not lose his head like a malefactor?[1] And after death he was more paraded than when aforetime riding in his chariot he used to exult in his dignity. And another, with a military command, attaining the same honor, fleeing the penalty of condemnation, perished miserably on the frontiers of Egypt and Libya, at last ending his life on the sands, since all the region through which he fled was waste and without habitation. And what can we say about that one of the generals and

[1] The allusion is to Rufinus, who fell A. D. 395.

consuls who is now living in disgrace in
the Colchian country, and who is kept alive
only by the generosity of the barbarians
there? And that one of the prefects, that
man invincible and lion-hearted as was sup-
posed, what an end his life had! For first
he beheld his own son beheaded; then he
himself also was doomed to die, but when
the noose had already been adjusted around
his neck, the royal clemency stayed the
hand of the executioner. And the old
man, after living a short time amid woes
and calamities, departed this life in disgrace, having found this the end of his
august consulship. And that other, so
much discussed by both men and women!
how last year he planned greater things
than the giants! Escaping his masters'
rods, he aspired to the rods of a consul.[1]
He acquired land to an amount not easy to

[1] *i. e.*, the fasces.

describe; but he was buried in only as much as the pitiful gave him.[1] Are not all such things then, according to the wise Preacher, Vanity of vanities ?[2]   And are not these political eminences like visions of baseless dreams, delighting for a little, then fleeting away; blooming and withering ? Let us therefore end our discourse at this point, and render glory to the Saviour.

[1] The allusion is to Eutropius, and supplies the only fixed date in the life of Asterius, who must have preached this sermon at the beginning of January, A. D. 400.

[2] Ecclesiastes 1 : 2.

V

ON DIVORCE

V

ON DIVORCE

ON the text from the Gospel according
to Matthew, whether it is lawful for a
man to put away his wife for every reason?[1]
A beautiful lesson is presented to the
Christians and the industrious in the con-
junction of these two days; I mean the
Sabbath and the Lord's Day, which revolv-
ing time brings round each week. These
days, as mothers or nurses of the church,
both assemble the people and seat the
priests before them as teachers. And they
lead both learners and teachers to care for
their souls. So the discourse of yesterday
is still ringing in my ears, and the things

[1] Matthew 19: 3.

that concerned us then linger in my memory. I behold the cross set up, according to
the prophecy of Isaiah, and the Lord's garments stained with blood, like the garments
of one who treads the wine-press;[1] and I
see the Saviour bearing in his right hand
the reward; and Solomon I behold exactly
arranging for us the balances and weights
to the best of his ability.[2]   And I pity the
debtor of the Gospel, who did not share
with his fellow servant the clemency which
he had received from his Lord, but by
thoughtlessness and harshness brought calamity again upon himself.[3] For with those
chapters we were yesterday busy as all of
you who were not inattentive know.

And to-day again the Spirit lays before
us many things, all beautiful, as many as
are on the table which you see. And I

[1] Isaiah 63: 1–3.   [3] Matthew 18: 28ff.
[2] Proverbs 11: 1.

have fixed my attention on the disputa-
tious and tempting Pharisees; and I have
pitied them exceedingly for the depravity of
their dispositions, inasmuch as they sought
to outwit even the Fountain of wisdom
by their questions and failed in their attempt; the divinity of the Only-begotten
ever turning their questions against themselves.   It was of them, as it seems to me,
that Isaiah prophesied, when he said, "I
am the Lord that turneth wise men back-
ward, and maketh their knowledge foolish;
that confirmeth the word of his servant." [1]
And again David says, "They flatter with
their tongue.   Hold them guilty, O God;
let them fall by their own counsels." [2]
But thanks be to them, hostile though they
were, that they moved Wisdom to answer,
in order that he might leave behind in
writing for us, his servants, instruction for

[1] Isaiah 44: 25.   [2] Psalm 5: 9, 10.

our profit. For, behold, marriage, the chief affair of human life, is regulated by him, and the limits of this union and the conditions of its dissolution are exactly determined. Let each one earnestly attend to the two ordinances of marriage, in order that women may be instructed as to their duties and men in the duties which belong to them.

"Whether it is lawful for a man to put away his wife for every reason?" This, then, is the problem of the Jews. I see the aim of their asking this question in the presence of the others. For since women are more ready to believe than men and are more susceptible to the magnificence of miracles, and inclined to the acceptance and belief of the divinity of Christ, (thus even behind the murderers who were dragging the Lord to the cross, was the multitude of women who bewailed his suf-

ferings, and, following the Saviour, piteously
lamented him)[1] in order that they might
lead him to offend and alienate all women,
the Jews, by their crafty question, laid a
trap and snare for him. But the Lord,
through the power of his divinity, seeing
what villainy they were devising, defeating
their treachery, and, at the same time, lay-
ing down beneficent rules of life, makes re-
ply, pleading the cause of women, and
sending away empty those hungry wolves
of Pharisees who in vain had snapped at
him with their questions. " The creation
itself," says he, " shows its aim to be union,
not separation."   The Creator was the first
bestower of the bride in marriage, since he
joined the first human beings in the
marriage bond, giving to those who should
come after, the inflexible ordinance of the
conjugal life, which must be recognized as

[1] Luke 23 : 27.

the law of God; and they who are thus associated with one another are no longer two, but one flesh, so that " What God hath joined together, let not man put asunder."

These things were spoken to the Pharisees; but do you hear them now, you who do such things as these: you who change your wives as readily as your garments; who build bridal chambers as often and as easily as you build booths for feasts; who marry money, and deal in women; who if provoked a little immediately write a bill of divorcement; you who leave many widows while you are yet alive; believe me, marriage is terminated only by death or adultery. For it is not as in the case of mistresses, a companionship for a few days only, nor a mere quest for pleasure, but like most other things is subject to rule and regulation. But in marriage, O man, both soul and body are united, so that dis-

position is mingled with disposition, and
flesh with flesh. How, then, are you
going to sever the bond of marriage
without suffering? How can you with-
draw from this union easily and without
pain, after taking your sister and wife not
as a servant of a few days, but as a partner
for life, a sister by reason of her formation
and creation,—for you were both made of
the same element of earth and of the same
substance,—and wife because of the conjugal union, because of the law of marriage?
What sort of a bond, then, are you about to
break, for you are bound by both law and
nature ; and how will you set at naught the
agreements which you made at marriage?
What sort of compacts do you think I
mean? Those made when the dowry had
been agreed upon, when with your own
hand you signed the roll, and set your seal
to the contract? These are strong indeed,

and possess stability enough, but I refer back to the utterance of Adam: "This is flesh of my flesh and bone of my bones, This shall be called my wife."[1] Not without reason is this utterance preserved in writing; for, uttered by the first man, it is the common covenant of men, made with the whole class of women, who are joined by law to their husbands. Do not be surprised if by what one has said, another is bound. For whatever happened in the beginning, in the case of those first created, has become the nature of their posterity.

If, then, the woman you have lightly divorced shall take the book of Genesis and drag you unto the Judge, who is both Judge and witness, tell me, what will you say? How will you repudiate your own utterance which you made in the name of

[1] Genesis 2: 23. The quotation does not agree exactly either with Heb. or Lxx.

God, which Moses, the servant of God, recorded, instead of some cheap notary? God gave Adam a wife without father and without mother; and for this reason, as a guardian he shielded the orphan. But now daughters strongly assert their mothers' rights against their unfeeling and undutiful husbands. So that from every point of view it is impossible for you to slight your wife with impunity, bound as you are by the ancient laws of God and the modern laws of men.

Let your wife's very helpfulness put you to shame. For she is a companion, a helper, a partner with whom to pass your life, and to bring children into the world, an aid in sickness, a comfort in distress, the guardian of the hearth, the custodian of the household goods, having the same sorrows, the same joys, sharing with you your wealth, if wealth be yours, or mitigating hard poverty, resourcefully and sturdily bearing up against its grievous consequences, and because of her marriage with you, enduring the toilsome rearing of children. And if perchance a change of fortune overtakes the husband, he overwhelmed thereby sinks into obscurity, and those who have been considered friends, measuring their friendship by the duration of his prosperity, desert him in his adversity, while the servants run away from both master and misfortunes. Only the wife is left, a partner of his distress, serving her husband amid manifold evils. She wipes away his tears, and heals his stripes if he be smitten. She follows him when he is led to prison ; and if permitted to enter with him, she cheerfully shares his confinement. But if even this be forbidden she remains at the door of the prison, like a dog devoted to his master.

I have known a woman who even cut off
her hair, and put on man's attire,—and
that gay-colored, in order that when her
husband fled and hid himself, she might
not be separated from him. And while
she seemed to be a slave, in truth she was
a slave of love. This life she lived for
many years, going from place to place, and
from wilderness to wilderness. Such a one,
too, we find the wife of most excellent
Job to be. For all had left him. With
the loss of his wealth his flatterers departed
from him. His friends, too, limited their
friendship by the duration of his prosperity.
If they were present at all, they came to
reproach, not to cheer him. Instead of
comforting him they aggravated his calamity. By reason of it, indeed, all his " miserable comforters "[1] uttered indignant complaints against him. But she alone, who

[1] Job 16 : 2.

had before lived in splendor, sat with her husband upon the dunghill, scraping off the discharge, and drawing the worms from his sores. Thus was she the partner of his life, not the sharer of his prosperity only; an inseparable friend, not a mere flatterer during his days of pleasure,—the only blessing that remained of all his good fortune and of all his intimates and kindred. So on account of her lofty and superlative affection for her husband, she fell even into the sin of blasphemy, counseling him to utter a blasphemous word against God so that he might die quickly and not be long punished, and that she might not see him in his ceaseless pains.[1]   For she took no account of her own misfortune of widowhood that would follow, but she cared for only one thing,—that her husband might escape from his insupportable existence. These

[1] Job 2 ; 9.

are the lessons which those who outrage
the ordinances of marriage should learn
from antiquity and from modern experience.

Now what can the man seeking divorce
say to this? And what sort of specious
defense of his own fickleness can he offer?
" My wife's disposition," he says, " is mean
and hateful, and her tongue is violent, and
her tastes are not domestic, and her house
is ill-managed." So be it. Granted. I
am so far persuaded, and accept it, like the
judges who are not very critical in hearing,
but are readily carried away by the invec-
tives of advocates. But tell me, when you
first married her, did you not know that
you were being joined to a human being?
And does anybody fail to see that to a
human being sin attaches? For perfection
is of God alone. And do you yourself,
then, never sin? Do you not cause your

wife pain by your conduct? Are you free
from all fault? Do you preserve the ordinance of wedlock in purity? Oh, how
many times, perhaps, your wife has endured
your drunken violence! How many ready
insults and shameful reproaches she has pa-
tiently suffered! And how many short-
comings of yours are kept secret, because
your wife has not published them! She
has borne with you when you were angry
without reason, and boiling with wrath;
and the free woman, your equal in station,
has remained silent like a slave from the
market. When you failed through poverty
or parsimony to furnish the necessaries of
life, though grieved, she did not reproach
you. Nay, further, when you came once
from a banquet, drunken and frenzied, she
did not cast you off, hating you for your
drunkenness, but with kindly forgiveness
she received you, and though you resisted,

she led you by the hand, and gently bathed your head, dizzied by the fumes of the wine, and guided you to the marriage bed, alone feeling sympathy, while the domestics were laughing and mocking at their master's drunken derangement. Yet you stalk about the neighborhood heartlessly accusing and misrepresenting your wife, that you may awaken sympathy for yourself and secure approval of your prospective divorce. Hard is the heart of such men, savage and cruel, sprung, as the proverb says, from oak or rock.[1] For wiping out the memory of all past kindnesses, they unfeelingly seek divorce. But who chops off a diseased limb, instead of healing it, and that, too, when no dangerous malady has attacked it, but when there is bright and certain pros-

---

[1] Odyssey 19 : 163, " You are not born of immemorial oak or rock " (Palmer). *Cf.* Clement of Alexandria, who quotes the verse, *Admonit. ad Gentes*, p. 18.

pect of restoration?   A blister has risen on
the hand; let us carefully attend to it.   A
boil has begun to annoy the foot; let us
reduce the swelling with liniment.   But if
we decline the attendance of physicians and
busy ourselves with amputation and the
knife in the case of each of the disordered
parts, before we have lived long we shall
have pruned ourselves of all our limbs.   But
not so, sirs.   Let there be some thought
even of the limbs.   Let the very services
of your wives put you to shame.   However
much you are provoked, compare the pain
of one child-birth with your grounds of
complaint, and you will find your crowd of
grievances outweighed.

Recall her good deeds of kindness:
nursing of the sick, companionship in misfortune, tearful entreaties in court on her
husband's behalf; leaving her parents and
the   ancestral   hearth,   and   following   a

stranger; selling her own property to
atone for her husband's insolence and re-
lieve his embarrassment. Let all this unite
you to her and prove a bond of affection,
propping up and making secure your un-
steady soul, as one braces a dilapidated
house. Let pity prevail, and let not inti-
macy and the association of a long life,
which makes even brute beasts inseparable,
be trodden under foot. For I have seen an
ox lowing piteously when he had wandered
away from his fellows and found himself
alone; and a sheep bleating in a glen and
scurrying over the mountains until it re-
joined the flock from which, while feeding,
it was parted. And a she-goat in this same
plight, no matter if as she runs she overtakes many flocks of goats, does not stop
until she finds her own flock and her own
herdsman.

Let us who are reasonable beings not be

found less susceptible to friendship than the brutes. And let us not hold a wife less precious than a fellow traveler, or a man, who on some slight pretext has suddenly become dear to us. You observe how men meeting one another even on the highways, and coming under the roof of the same inn, or under some spreading tree, as a shelter in summer from the noonday heat, make the chance meeting the occasion of genuine friendship; and when they come to the place where their ways diverge, they do not part from one another without emotion, but stand and with tears in their eyes look earnestly upon one another, while each gives mementoes to the other to carry with him. And after going a little way, they turn back again, and call to each other, invoking good fortune upon each other. Does a little time like this cement a friendship so closely that separation be-

comes difficult and is only effected by
absolute necessity, and will you think as
lightly of the partner of your life, as of a
broken dish, or a cheap cloak spoiled on a
journey, or a Maltese lap-dog that has es-
caped the house? Where is that attachment
that was formed at first? Where the sharing of one bed, the bond of law, the power
of constant and protracted association,
which, as the saying is, and experience
proves,—becomes a second nature? You
have snapped them all asunder more easily
than Samson the cords of the Philistines.[1]

But the man who is wise and guards his
attachment does not easily forget his wife
even after she has departed this life; but
he cherishes the children that she leaves as
a trust common to him and her and sees
in them the departed one. For one of the
children preserves the tones of his mother's

[1] Judges 16: 12,

voice; another possesses most of her features;
another is like her in disposition. Thus
the father has impressed upon him, with
many living and striking likenesses of his
wife before him, the immortal character of
his union with her. For this reason, he
takes no thought of pleasure. He does not
to-day heap up a grave and shortly thereafter furnish a nuptial chamber. He does
not hasten from tears and groans to the
marriage dance. He does not exchange
his black and mourning garb for a wedding suit. He does not lead a second wife to
the marriage bed, still warm, of her who is
departed, nor does he give a stepmother,
hateful name, to his children. But he
imitates the strange yet natural devotion of
the turtle-dove. For they say that that
bird, when separated from its mate, devotes
itself to perpetual widowhood, and is very different from the common dove, as far as mating

again is concerned. So, then, let reproaches come thick and fast upon the husband who seeks divorce, and let the charges of ingratitude, falling thicker than snowflakes, pelt him.

But if he put forward a charge of adultery, and offer this as the ground of his separation, I will at once become the advocate of the injured man, and directing my discourse against the adulteress, will take my stand beside the husband, no longer his foe, but his valiant ally, commending him who flees the treacherous woman, and severs the tie which bound him to an asp and a viper. For the Creator of all is the first to absolve this man as justly indignant, and right in driving the plague from his house and hearth. For marriage exists for these two things, love and offspring, neither of which is compatible with adultery. For there is no love when affection turns towards another; and honor in bringing children into the world is destroyed, when their parentage is made doubtful. The things that contribute to this sin have been duly mentioned under another head. But pray let both parties to the marriage contract practise self-control,—the unbroken bond of wedlock.   For where the honor of marriage is maintained, there is, of necessity, affection and peace, with no vulgar and unlawful desire to excite the soul, and expel legitimate and righteous love.

This law of self-control is not ordained by God for women alone, but for men also. But they who give heed to secular lawgivers, and leave to men the unrestricted license of adultery, while they are stern judges and teachers of the sanctity of women, are themselves shamelessly licentious. Healers of others, according to the proverb, they are yet themselves full of sores.[1] If any one upbraids them with these offenses, they offer a subtle and playful defense. For men, they say, even if they approach many women, do their own hearth no harm; but women, if they sin, introduce alien heirs into their houses and families. But let the sophistical inventors of this frivolous justification of their conduct know that they themselves are overturning other hearths and homes. For the women with whom they associate are surely the daughters or wives of somebody; and in any case there will be found either a marriage plotted against, or a parent wronged who has begotten and reared a daughter, hoping to have a virgin for the bridal chamber, but whose fond expectation has been thwarted by the robbers of her virtue. If the wretch is a father, let him think on the feelings of a father who

[1] *Cf.* Euripides, Frag. 1071.

has been thus disappointed; if a husband, let him imagine himself the injured man. For usually it is well that each one judge the affairs of another as he wishes another to judge his own. And if any, heeding the law of the Romans, consider fornication permissible, they make a dreadful mistake, not knowing that God lays down law in one way, while men make statutes in another. Listen to Moses, as he proclaims the will of God, and utters bitter condemnation against fornicators.[1] Listen to Paul when he says : " Fornicators and adulterers God will judge."[2] Other teachers will not be able to save you in the time of retribution, but, trembling and filled with consternation, they shall melt away. Plato, the professor of laws, shall appear to you then ignorant and untaught, and that weighty voice, which assumed authority over all

[1] Deuteronomy 22 : 22.   [2] Hebrews 13 : 4.

lawgivers, will be humbled when he and they shall see the lovers of the body to whom they have wickedly permitted license, dragged forth to punishment. And assuredly they who have not forbidden others, have first involved themselves in the sin, and are found liable to a twofold charge, both for what they themselves have done, and because they have allowed others to be licentious. Let those, therefore, whose purpose it is to live with the very purest wives, make their own manner of life a model for their spouses, in order that they may maintain in the home a worthy rivalry in virtue.